CONNECTION EXPANSION

CONNECTION EXPANSION

You Are One Connection Away From Massive Success In Your Life And Business

DEVIN SIZEMORE

Devin Sizemore
devin@devinsizemore.com
https://devinsizemore.com/

Connection Expansion, Devin Sizemore —1st ed.

TESTIMONIALS

"Devin has helped me implement his system into my business, and helped me focus on the true value of my relationships and my network. The concept of "many to many" versus "one to one" relationships is probably foreign to most people, but if you can learn and embrace these principles, the end result will be a 100x return in your referral business!"

—Chris O'Sullivan, President of Stillmeadow Partners

"I've had the privilege of knowing Devin Sizemore for three years, a friendship that began through a referral from a mutual friend. From the very start, Devin provided immense value by connecting me with others who could add significant value to my business and our clients. His support has only grown since then. The results and impact of using Devin's Connection Expansion System™ are real, transforming my network into a powerhouse of opportunity. If you're serious about scaling your networking efforts and unlocking the true potential of your professional relationships, this book is your guide."

—Chuck Cooper, President of Whitewater Consulting and author of The Family Business Blueprint & Unprecedented

"If you don't have a way to predictably generate leads you don't have a business. You're just getting lucky. Devin explains in this book how to generate leads in a predictable way that are 100% referral and relationship-based. This is a scalable game changer."

—Chris Williams, Founder of Group Coach Nation

"I met Devin the week I started my business. I had no idea how to go about building a network, truthfully, I only had a vague notion that I should build a network. At that time, he already had an impressive "resume" and I was able to learn about Connection Expansion and how to build meaningful connections very quickly. Today, 10 years later, my agency has grown into a million-dollar business and I have never made a single cold call, which is fortunate because I hate cold calling. I have also made lifelong friends because of this system and many of my days are filled with great conversations. Since I started my business there are 5 key people that I can thank for my success and Devin Sizemore is at the top of that list."

—Aaron Ware, Owner of Aware Benefits

"Being happy about getting to work with Devin on my networking is putting it too mildly. Working with Devin helped me reimagine what networking looks like. I like the 'process over results' framework he talks about that empowers us to work on only what we can control. Oftentimes we know that -- but don't know how our outreach activities actually mirror that internalized concept. Devin gives you the language, mindset, and framework to do that. Working with Devin gave me personalized insights for my context and I've already started to see the fruit of how my business relationships are responding to this new way of doing things."

—Eric Saar, Owner and CEO of Slingshot Media Consulting

"Building strong relationships and referral partners is crucial to growing your network and business. I've known Devin Sizemore for over a decade, and I started implementing his system early on. Over the years, I've refined my approach and learned the immense value of expanding key relationships for personal and professional growth. Today, over 50% of my business comes from warm leads generated through deep connections with high-level connectors. This book offers practical insights into identifying and nurturing high-value relationships that can significantly enhance your career or business. It introduces a unique approach that moves beyond traditional networking, focusing on building many-to-many relationships. The Connection Expansion System™ is a key element in this guide, providing a scalable framework that generates consistent referrals. It's not just theory—this system offers actionable steps, including specific language and scripts, to help you succeed. By leveraging the value in every relationship and applying this strategy, you can scale your networking efforts and naturally attract qualified prospects. This approach turns your network into a powerful engine for long-term success and growth."

—Keenan Polan, Director of Sales at the Barracuda Championship

"Just working with you causes my organizational skills to uplevel. I'm super grateful for this business relationship that we do have. It has caused me to uplevel, so your excellence has caused my excellence to uplevel for sure. I have lots of connections from you which I deeply appreciate. There are so many incredible humans that you're connected to it's not even funny how you do what you do. So I appreciate you for all those connections."

—Wendy Paquette, Quantum Timeline Shifter

"I just wanted to say how grateful I am for all you taught me. It will pay dividends for years to come. Honestly for the rest of my life."

—Colt Vines, Real Estate Agent

DEDICATION

This book is dedicated to all you people out there who wake up each day, put on your armor, and fight for yourself, your family, your employees, and everyone you impact. Some days the task can feel daunting, but nothing is more rewarding. This book is for you. I hope to ease your burden and help you find connections that unlock massive success for you and your business.

CONTENTS

FOREWORD

In a world increasingly driven by technology and digital interactions, the value of human connections cannot be overstated. Devin Sizemore, an entrepreneur, and business leader understands this better than most. His journey, filled with a rich tapestry of professional experiences, has taught him a simple yet profound truth: our network is our most valuable asset.

Devin has built his career on the foundation of connecting people and their respective opportunities. Known for his uncanny ability to bring together the right individuals at the right time, Devin has earned the reputation of a "super connector." Whether through his business ventures, coaching, or speaking engagements, Devin consistently demonstrates how forging meaningful connections can create synergies that propel both individuals and organizations toward success. His philosophy is rooted in the belief that genuine relationships, built on trust and mutual benefit, are the key to unlocking both personal and professional growth.

In this book, Devin delves deep into the art and science of networking. He offers practical strategies and insightful anecdotes that illuminate how anyone can leverage their connections to achieve their goals. But more than that, he challenges us to rethink the way we approach our relationships, urging us to see each interaction as an opportunity to make a meaningful impact.

I have experienced firsthand the extraordinarily accurate and valuable connections that Devin routinely makes as we have participated in several mastermind and mentoring groups together. I invite you to discover the practical steps you can take to unlock the power of your network as you read Connection Expansion.

Enjoy!

—Kevin Petersen, Entrepreneur and Investor

INTRODUCTION

Whenever I ask business owners about their best source of new business, the answer is almost always the same: referrals. Referrals are pre-sold prospects who already view you as the solution to their problem, making them easier to close. Who doesn't want that?

However, when I probe further and ask how many referrals they receive on a daily, weekly, or monthly basis, their response is often vague or unclear.

I call this "The Referral Dilemma." Business owners clearly desire more referrals, but they lack a system that consistently and predictably generates them. If you're reading this book, you likely haven't fully solved this problem, leaving significant untapped potential in your network.

Whether you have a large contact list, a strong social following, or a database of people who know you, the Connection Expansion System™ will show you how to extract 100x the value from these resources. If your network is limited, this system will help you grow it in alignment with your strengths and gamify the process, making it enjoyable even if you dislike sales.

What if you could find just one high-value connection within your network that consistently introduced you to highly aligned prospects, referral partners, and resources that benefit both you and your business? I'm willing to bet that you already have three or more of these connections—you simply haven't realized it yet or figured out how to tap into their full potential. In this book, I will walk you through the exact steps to identify, communicate with, and position yourself to tap into the full power of these relationships, all while continuously adding new contacts to your network.

I would hate to see you, like many other business owners, continue to recognize the value in referrals, but struggle to generate them consistently and predictably. You're likely really good at what you do and offer a product or service that more people NEED. Let's get you plugged into a proven system that puts you back in control, allowing you to expand your business and reach the vision and goals you have set for yourself.

You can access additional resources, templates, and content related to the strategies talked about in this book at www.ConnectionExpansionBook.com.

To rapidly expand your network with high-quality connections that generate consistent referrals, keep reading. I'll introduce you to the Connection Expansion System™.

CHAPTER 1

The Referral Dilemma

> *"People influence people. Nothing influences people more than a recommendation from a trusted friend. A trusted referral influences people more than the best broadcast message. A trusted referral is the Holy Grail of advertising."*
>
> — Mark Zuckerberg

What is your best source of new business?

Anytime I ask this question, especially in a room full of business owners, the answers are usually the same: referrals.

This makes complete sense—you're already pre-sold to a prospect and positioned as the person who has the product or service to solve their problem. Typically, referrals are much easier to close and require a lot less effort to move through your sales cycle.

I usually then follow up with a few other questions:

- How many referrals do you get daily, weekly, or monthly?

- Are the numbers of referrals you receive predictable?
- Do you feel like you're getting referrals when you ask, or do they feel random?

Often the consensus is that referrals are blessings when they show up, but there is not a lot of predictability.

A quick search shows that businesses typically have 2 - 5% of their total customer base sending them referrals. That statistic alone should help you realize the huge untapped potential in your customer list. I don't know about you, but even 5% doesn't seem like the standard I want to hold myself to. What about identified referral partners? What about the other contacts in your database? What about everyone else you run into on a daily or weekly basis? Are you struggling to find a predictable way to generate new referrals?

Thus, the Referral Dilemma is born. You, like many other business owners, see the value in referrals yet often lack a system to consistently and predictably generate them.

Capturing The Real Potential

A lot of the conversations about generating more referrals revolve around the question: *How do I get my active clients to refer me to more prospects?*. There are some great strategies for reaching out to active clients, identifying "raving fans" or "advocates" (common terminology in these conversations), and then motivating them or asking them to make high-quality referrals to your business.

However, even the most successful of these customer referral campaigns still results in only 5% of your customers referring business to you. The other problem with this approach is that you're focusing your time and effort on a one-to-one relationship, hoping that one person connects you to another.

As we explore marketing and sales strategies my ultimate goal for you and your team is to show you how to use your time and energy to find, add value to, and nurture relationships that give you access to many of your ideal clients, not just one potential client. As we explore the concepts below, we'll focus on how they apply to relationships, which will be at the core of everything we discuss in this book.

One-To-One Relationships

This is pretty straightforward: you focus your efforts on speaking directly to one prospect in the hopes of converting them into a client. This is great if you can scale it for your product or service, clearly understand your key performance indicators (KPIs) , and have real clarity into your cost per client acquisition. However, when building one-to-one relationships, you'll likely have to keep fueling the machine to generate results. These types of strategies typically cost more and require a lot of work for a limited return on investment.

One-To-Few Relationships

These are opportunities where you can speak to a few potential clients in one space. Client referral strategies typically fall into this bucket as each client may introduce you to a few prospects (if you are lucky). Additionally, many referral or channel partner relationships end up here (for the remainder of the book I am going to use "referral partner"). Often, fewer referrals are made than the referral partner promised. Like one-to-one strategies, one-to-few relationships typically take continuous work and often yield a limited ROI.

One-To-Many Relationships

These are usually relationships with referral partners. Here, you invest time and energy into developing relationships that give you access to many potential clients. This is where the real magic happens. Once you've properly nurtured one-to-many relationships, they continue to produce connections and referrals. With enough of these relationships, you can focus more on nurturing them rather than continually generating new ones. As a result, you will see that your return on investment begins to increase dramatically.

Many-to-Many Relationships

This is the next step in relationship building and where you'll find exponential growth in the relationships you're cultivating. Many-to-many relationships are those that give you access to many referral partners who then have access to many clients. This level of relationship increases your ROI more than any of the other relationship types. With enough of these relationships in place, your network will grow itself, continually introducing you to new connections that you can nurture.

By the end of this book, my goal is to show you how to implement the exact system that hundreds of business professionals have used to generate connections, resulting in new clients, million dollar partnerships, speaking opportunities, podcast invites, exclusive event invitations, and much more. It's amazing what the power of one high-value connection can do for your life and business. In fact, I bet you're simply one connection away from massive success in your life and business.

Why stop there? Let's build a machine that will open doors to many high-value connections for you. I'll walk you through how to set up and implement the Connection Expansion System™. This is the system that will allow you to predictably generate many-to-many relationships and referrals for your business.

Referrals vs. Connections

It's important to define some key terminology early in this book, so we're on the same page. Let's start by examining the difference between a referral and a connection.

A "referral" will be defined as an introduction to a prospective client.

A "connection" will be defined as any introduction made to you or your organization with no assumptions about what that connection will turn into.

We will dive much deeper into this in later chapters, but keep the distinction between referral and connection in mind as you read.

A Core Challenge To Developing Many-To-Many Relationships

There's a saying that I recommend you write on a sticky note and put it somewhere you will see it regularly. This saying is at the core of *why* the system we're going to discuss was born - ***"Everybody Wants To Buy, Nobody Wants To Be Sold".***

You need to keep this saying in mind because as soon as you start "selling", you will destroy the system you are creating and get limited to no results.

Everybody you are "selling" to has been trained to consume (purchase) goods and services. Yet we all know how it feels when we're being 'sold' to. To succeed in sales, we need to appeal to the buyer's natural impulse to purchase, without letting on that we're selling to them.

This quote also points to the foundational principles of consultative selling, also known as needs-based selling. This is a sales approach that focuses on building relationships with customers and addressing their needs through open dialogue. In this approach, sales representatives act as advisors, recommending solutions based on a customer's needs and pain points, rather than pushing a specific product. The goal is to form lasting connections with customers and solve their problems. Although this book won't go too deep into sales strategies, a lot of what works for consultative selling is also at the core of The Connection Expansion System™.

You Are Setting Yourself Up For Disappointment

Another challenge I find with a lot of the approaches to asking for more referrals is *how* people are asking for them. When I am out networking, in a one-to-one meeting, or even when I am the customer, the ask typically sounds something like this:

"I am looking to connect with [INSERT IDEAL CLIENT PROFILE/S here]."

Sometimes, the asker adds a statement explaining why this client profile is beneficial for them.

Now don't get me wrong, you should have a clear picture of your client profiles (we'll revisit this in Chapter 3). The challenge is that we then need to refer back to the saying, "everybody wants to buy, nobody wants to be sold". When you make this ask, you're asking me to look in my network, identify people who fit the profile you described, and then introduce them to you so that you can "sell" to them. In most cases, these referrals feel forced or just don't happen, because I don't want to position someone to be "sold".

There are times where having this information is very handy. I might have someone in my network or end up in a conversation where your product or service is an exact fit for someone I am talking to. In these cases, you've done your job, and I'll feel great for making a referral where everybody wins.

But by providing an answer that is framed around your ideal client profile, you dramatically limit my ability to identify potential connections for you in my network.

By the end of this book I will help you change the way you ask for referrals and expand your language to ask for connections, greatly increasing the number of both you receive.

A Lot of Untapped Value

There are limited instances when I meet a business owner who has a robust client referral program *and* a fruitful referral partner program. Even in those instances, I find there is a lot of untapped value in their network or database.

This is typically because the focus on who makes a good referral partner is too narrow. We will explore this further in Chapter 3 when I walk you through the Connection Expansion Exercise™.

If you have a large contact list, a strong social following, a list of clients, and a database of people who know of you, then the Connection Expansion System™ will show you how to get 100x the value you are getting out of those lists.

If you don't have a strong network, database, or social following, the Connection Expansion System™ will empower you to grow your network in a way that aligns with your strengths and gamifies the process so, even if you hate sales, you can have fun and succeed with the system.

If you want to rapidly expand your network via high-quality connections that will position you for a steady stream of ongoing referrals, jump into Chapter 2 where I'll Introduce you to the Connection Expansion System™.

CHAPTER 2

The Connection Expansion System™

"Organize around business functions, not people. Build systems within each business function. Let systems run the business and people run the systems. People come and go but the systems remain constant."

— Michael Gerber

Making high-value connections to generate consistent referrals is the primary goal for most people implementing the Connection Expansion System™. However, there are a lot of additional benefits to having a high-value network.

What if…

- You never had to market for an open position at your company because your networking strategy aligned you with the right people at the right time or could be tapped into when needed?
- You could launch a business for 50% of what it should cost because of the untapped value in your network and

your ability to bring specific resources to the project quickly?

- You could save money and have a better experience while traveling because you know people who are traveling to the same place at the same time or have property where you're planning to travel?
- You were invited to exclusive, invite-only opportunities with no other way to access them?
- You could get a $125,000 year job offer and not have to compete for the position?
- You secure an ideal internship without having to apply or find the ideal intern without having to screen candidates and sift through applications?
- You could find an attorney and have them take a call within 24 hours for a very important and timely matter, even when all the attorneys in that area of practice are booked out for months?
- You never had to search for service providers like realtors, lenders, or insurance agents again because they were either already in your network or you could get a half dozen referrals in a matter of minutes?

You may have noticed some of these situations might not apply to you, but they may apply to your staff, your spouse, your kids, or people you mentor or coach. The Connection Expansion System™ creates high-value networks. But how you use these networks really depends on your current goals and needs. Please note that all of the above are based on real results and experiences from using the system. These are just a sampling of the ways that having a high-value network can provide additional opportunities and resources when and if you need them.

Disclaimer - It Takes Time And Effort

Before we dive too deep, I want to properly set your expectations. Yes, there is tremendous value that can come out of this system, but it will take time and it will take effort. Most of the businesses I work with begin to see real traction around 90 and 120 days into implementing the system. Now, there are some parts of the system that should and will have an immediate impact, but the big results come from the compounding effect. The best part is that once implemented, the system will continue to scale exponentially and deliver results long into the future.

Exponential Growth Through Strategic Connection Building

Let me give you a high level overview of how the system helps you scale exponentially. Say you use the catch up script (shared in Chapter 4: Networking For Connections) to book three Connection Meetings. You then add value to those connections by introducing each of them to 3 - 5 strategic people that add value to them. This then gives you the ability to follow up with the 12 - 18 connections (*the three original connections plus the 3 - 5 people you introduce them to*) and see how the introductions went.

Now you have permission to follow up with 12 - 18 people, which will likely lead to you booking more Connection Meetings with the people you haven't met with in awhile. In addition, because you're adding value strategically to all those connections, there is a high-probability that some of those people will make connections for you. Let's assume that 25% of the people you helped introduce someone to make one strategic introduction for you. Now you will have 3 - 4 new connections that you can have connection meetings with, and the cycle begins again.

The things I want you to take away from the above are:

- With 3 connections you can scale rapidly. Everyone has at least three people they can meet with.
- Even if you only have a 25% success rate for getting new people connected to you, the system works. I have an over 75% success rate with an average of two connections per person.
- The system fuels the system. The more proficient you get at the various parts, the faster it will scale.

Gaining A Competitive Advantage

Although I've been an entrepreneur since I could walk, I did hold a corporate position for a few years. In my position, I was in charge of growing a branch for a national publicly traded PEO (professional employer organization).

The company had built an extensive and very successful referral network. Their approach, like that of the other area managers, was to target commercial insurance brokers as strong referral partners. This approach made sense given the core services that we were selling, however it had some drawbacks. First, every other PEO was targeting the same referral partners, leading to conversations around why one company was better than the other. This meant most discussions were competitive in nature.

I used the Connection Expansion Exercise™ and the Connection Expansion System™ to identify other strategic partners in the market that had access to our ideal clients. I then booked as many meetings as I could with this expanded list of potential referral partners.

Fast forward a couple of years and I had built out a couple hundred referral partnerships (while most branches had a couple dozen). Over 80% of our new business came from "non-traditional" referral partners, with accountants and B2B sales professionals proving particularly valuable. This led to over $30 million in growth for the branch, making it the top performing branch in our region. This success was largely due to the expansion and nurturing of our referral network.

I share this story to show how you, like many others, might be missing an opportunity to set yourself apart from the competition. The Connection Expansion System™ will help you find opportunities for yourself and your business that your competitors are not paying attention to.

A System Built On Core Principles

As I have built and refined the Connection Expansion System™ over the last decade for myself and hundreds of clients, there have been many minor adjustments that have increased the overall results, but the core principles have always been the same:

- Always Add Value
- Control What You Can Control

- There Is Value In Every Relationship
- Never Make Assumptions About A Connection
- You Have To Train By Doing

Always Add Value

I see so often where business owners and sales professionals are so focused on closing deals that they forget to add value along the way. I also see this in marketing. Our goal with marketing is to get people to raise their hand so we can sell to them—really? Your goal with marketing is to get people into your pipeline so that you can nurture them and then yes, you ultimately would like to sell to them.

What if those people you add to your pipeline aren't ideal clients, but have access to them? Your current strategy could be eliminating or alienating those individuals, costing you upside potential. We will explore this more in the next chapter.

Your goal when it comes to building any relationship is to add value to the relationship *as quickly and in as many ways as possible*. When I say "add value" people often jump straight to their product or service. Yes, that is one way to add value, but that should not be our focus unless someone expresses an interest in what we are selling. Other ways to add value are through solving problems, providing education, making connections, or providing other resources that the relationship may need.

I personally prefer making 2 - 4 quality connections as fast as I can in any given relationship (as demonstrated in the exponential growth section above). I want you to think about how you are adding value to those around you. Are you actually adding value or are you simply trying to sell your product or service?

I promise that if you shift your approach to adding value as quickly as you can (not your product or service), you will find that your network will greatly expand and you will attract others to join in a big way!

Control What You Can Control

Think through the stages in your ideal client's buying process. If you are a service-based business then those stages may look something like the following: 1st Meeting, Discovery Meeting, Proposal Creation, Proposal Presentation, Negotiation, Contracting, Onboarding.

If you are a product-based business, the stages may be something like: Information Gathering, Educating, Alignment On Your USP, Urgency & Scarcity, Purchase, and Upsell.

No matter what business you have, there are stages that your ideal client will move through before buying your product or service. To take this a step further, clearly define what each stage means and what triggers a prospect to move to the next stage. For example, let's define the 1st Meeting as a "get to know you meeting". Later we will define these as Connection Meetings and go deeper into why and how to conduct them. This is not a sales meeting, it is simply an opportunity to build a relationship and determine where there might be more value.

The Discovery Meeting would be the 1st meeting with a potential client who has expressed interest in your product or service. In this section, I'll use a service-based example. If you have a product business, you should see many places where you could define similar "controllables" for your stages. Let's use these stages as we move through this conversation: 1st Meeting, Discovery Meeting, Proposal Creation, Proposal Presentation, Negotiation, Contracting, Onboarding.

To schedule 1st meetings you need to meet new people. One common way of doing this is to go to networking events. Now, as a successful business owner, you may feel that you have moved beyond this. I get it. The events can be exhausting and feel like a waste of time. You could also book several 1st meetings just by reaching out to your current database. But for the sake of this journey and this book's chapter structure,let's talk about a networking event.

When I ask people what their goal is when attending a networking event, I often hear, " to meet potential clients." But why limit yourself to meeting only potential clients and put pressure on yourself to identify them in an environment that forces quick communications? Your goal should simply be to meet people. This is where we get into *controlling what you can control*.

- You can control whether or not you show up to the event.
- You can then control how many conversations you have with people at the event.
- You can also control getting their business cards so that you can control the follow-up process.

- You can then control how fast your follow-up is and what wording you use.
- You can then control how often you follow up and how you nurture the relationship.
- You can then control the structure of the 1st meeting.
- You can then control how you follow up from a 1st meeting.
- You can then control when and how you add value to the relationship.
- You can then control how you nurture that relationship long-term.

Hopefully, you are starting to see a theme here.

So often I see sales teams being held accountable to KPIs (key performance indicators) that they can't control. You need to hold your team accountable to the things you know with confidence that they can control. If they do what they can control at a certain scale, then you know that they will have enough qualified leads in their pipeline.

Yes, I want to track meetings and the number of deals closed at each stage. But, let's get one thing straight—you cannot force a prospect to buy from you. No level of ninja sales tactics will make a prospect buy from you if the time isn't right, they don't have the budget, or there isn't a clear alignment in the value proposition.

When you take this pressure off yourself and your team, building a thriving pipeline and high-impact network is much more enjoyable.

There Is Value In Every Relationship

I recently spoke with a business owner who had just returned from a large local trade show. As I listened to their takeaways and reviewed their prospect list, something stood out to me. The business owner kept saying things like, "I talked to a few people that *seem* like they need our product or service," or "I would try and move through the conversation in a way that would help me determine *if they were a prospect,*" or "I would look for indications that they *needed* our product or service." Now, I'm not suggesting you shouldn't do these things, however, as we talked through the conversations that business owner and his team had at the tradeshow, it became clear that they missed a ton of opportunities to find and build meaningful relationships. They were focused on the short-game of landing new clients. I want you to focus on the long-game, which will generate exponentially more results.

You never know what someone's spouse, parents, or siblings do. You don't know what organizations they belong to, either now or in the past. You don't know what their previous careers or businesses were. You don't know what else they might own. You don't know who they might know. In fact, in a short conversation at a networking event or tradeshow, it is safe to say you barely know anything about the person you just talked to. How could you possibly make an assumption about the value of that relationship? You can't.

The Hidden Value Exercise

Every time I am doing a presentation and I get push back about the core principle, There Is Value In Every Relationship, I walk the room through this exercise.

I first ask everyone in the room to give me a very obscure "ask" for a type of connection that would be valuable for them. Typically, it takes a few people to answer before we find an ask that the room agrees is obscure. In one example, I had a student say that they were very interested in ham radios and would love to learn more about that industry. Another time, I had a business owner say they wanted to learn to fly a plane. I've had someone say they were interested in doing work in the reggae industry. I've even had someone say they wanted to connect with someone who had visited Turkmenistan.

Once we agree that the ask seems obscure, I then ask everyone in the room if they, or someone in their network, could add value to the person based on their ask. The majority of the time when I do this exercise, there is at least one hand that goes up in the room. If a hand doesn't go up, I usually share a few connections I could make that I think would be valuable for the person based on their ask. I then ask the room if those examples trigger any ideas for potential connections and 100 percent of the time, a hand will go up with someone who can make a valuable connection for the asker.

I share this exercise because, as I hope you'll discover throughout this book, there is often hidden value within your current network, new connections you're making, and the events you attend. Your job now is to equip yourself to find the value in every relationship.

It's important to stop crippling your pipeline and overall network growth by weeding out potential relationships based on a limited understanding of their potential value.

Never Make Assumptions About A Connection

This leads to another core principle. Never make assumptions about a connection (person). As the old saying goes, "You know what happens when you assume...you make an ass out of you and me." Anytime you find yourself assuming something, recognize it in the moment and shift your perspective to "What don't I know?" You *must always* remain curious, and you'll be amazed at the opportunities that present themselves.

You Have To Train By Doing

The last core principle is to train people to do what you want them to do by modeling the actions yourself. In the case of the Connection Expansion System™, we want the people in our network to make frequent high-value connections to new people for us. If that's the goal, then we must excel at making meaningful connections ourselves, demonstrating the process for those in our network. This principle will also come into play when we talk about the questions you ask when networking, how you frame the Connection Meeting, and how you nurture relationships long-term. By following the system as outlined, you will be teaching your network to do the same, which will in turn, level up what the system is doing for you!

An Overview of What's To Come

The Connection Expansion System™ has pieces that touch on all the steps of building a relationship. For the rest of the book, I will walk you through all of those pieces.

- In Chapter 3 I will walk you through the Connection Expansion Exercise™. This will help you build a list specific to you that will help you scale from one-to-one relationships to many-to-many relationships.
- In Chapter 4 I will walk you through how you should approach making new connections in a way that will give you the most probability of finding high-value connections.
- In Chapter 5 I will give you the exact process that myself and my clients have used to book thousands of meetings with very little friction.
- In Chapter 6 I will walk you through how to approach your Connection Meetings to get the most out of them and position yourself for long-term success.
- In Chapter 7 I will share with you the best practices and exact scripts used to follow up from your Connection Meetings and how this system can start to exponentially scale.
- In Chapter 8 I will share with you how you can nurture your network, no matter what type of connection, for long-term success and to fill your calendar quickly when and if you or your team need to.

- In Chapter 9 we will dive into the tools and processes that support the overall system.

By the end of the book, you should have a very clear understanding of how you can unlock the potential of your network and the various shifts you make to have more impact with what you are already doing.

Let's begin with the Connection Expansion Exercise™.

CHAPTER 3

The Connection Expansion Exercise™

"You can never judge a book by its cover."

— George Eliot

Let me introduce you to the Connection Expansion Exercise™. The goal of this exercise is to help give you clarity on how to shift from one-to-one relationships to many-to-many relationships. In addition to shifting to a focus on many-to-many relationships, there are also benefits to exploring different types of relationships when we explore how to get to our ideal clients.

I would recommend you take notes as you are moving through each of the steps below. It will help you see trends and opportunities. Focus on one ideal client profile at a time as you are working through the process before applying it to another profile.

If you ever get stuck while developing your list, try a quick online search using phrases like "Where do [insert ideal client] gather, spend money, or seek education?". You can narrow the search down based on the area you are feeling stuck in. There are no right or wrong answers, your goal is to start to realize the number of connections that have access to your ideal client and hopefully identify some that others in your industry may not be leveraging.

Ideal Client Profile: Who Do You Want To Sell To?

You should have a pretty clear picture of your ideal client profiles or avatars. There are lots of names for what this may look like, but at the end of the day, you need a detailed understanding of who you're targeting.

There are a couple of things that I would recommend you confirm before moving beyond this step. When you look at your client profiles, make sure you are focused on the clients who are easiest to work with *and* likely to buy your highest-margin service. There's no point in putting a lot of time and energy into building a high-value network that puts you in front of less-than-ideal clients. Make sure you are very clear on who you want to meet when the opportunity for a well-aligned prospect meeting arises.

Again, keep one of these ideal client profiles in mind as you work your way through the next steps.

Vendors: Where Does Your Ideal Client Spend Money?

Here is where we expand our view of who we should be targeting. I want you to have a clear picture of the one ideal client you have identified. Now, think about where your ideal clients spend money.

If you are struggling, pull up your personal or business bank account and look at what you spend money on. Do you think your ideal clients spend money in the same places? You'll likely be able to expand this list just by thinking about where you spend money.

We target vendors because they already have a financial relationship with your ideal client. That means trust is already established, and the client is accustomed to spending money with them—leading to a higher likelihood of successfully closed referrals. These vendors also likely work with a number of your ideal clients, allowing you to scale from one-to-one to one-to-many relationships.

For example, if you're a real estate agent building a list of vendors, many realtors I talk to first think of mortgage lenders and insurance agents. The issue is that every other realtor has the same answer. The goal is to expand your list so you can see opportunities to find referral sources and strategic partnerships that others in the industry are likely not paying attention to. Examples could include pest control, solar sales, alarm companies, cleaning companies, and other home service providers. If you're targeting first-time homebuyers, then childcare facilities or new parent education companies might be a great addition to your list.

Before moving on, try to compile a list of at least a dozen vendors that your ideal client regularly spends money with.

Education: Where do your ideal clients seek education?

The next list is where our ideal clients seek education. If your clients need continuing education for licenses, this list should be pretty easy. Don't stop there though, think about other places they might seek education. Are there trade organizations they belong to? How about personal development, leadership training, or sales training programs they attend?

Think about authors, podcasts, and training websites they may follow as well. These individuals and organizations are great because your ideal clients already trust them to provide valuable education. Should they refer your ideal client to you, there's already a strong foundation of trust behind the recommendation.

If you are a B2C business, this step can be more challenging, but it is still possible. For example, if you are targeting parents then you may look for new parent courses, family finance courses, relationship courses, etc. There are always things that individuals seek education for.

You could also explore hobbies your ideal client enjoys and identify ways they might seek education for those hobbies.

Ideally, you should have a list of 3 - 5 people or organizations you believe your ideal client seeks education from.

Gather: Where Do Your Ideal Clients Gather Together?

Now think about where your ideal clients gather. This list likely includes some of the places that your ideal clients seek education. Again, let's think beyond that. These may be industry events or organizations. If you are targeting senior citizens, this may be bingo night, or other events focused on seniors. If you are targeting young professionals, this could be local young professional groups. If you are targeting parents, then this might be parent-teacher associations or youth sports organizations.

Your ideal clients are gathering, it is your job to figure out where. Ideally, you should have 3 - 5 places where your ideal client is gathering before moving to the next list.

Influence: Who Has Influence Over Your Ideal Clients?

These are usually thought leaders, coaches, or mentors in your ideal client's industry. These are the people or organizations that your ideal clients lean into to stay up-to-date on trends, and are the people or organizations who inspire your ideal clients in some way. An example of this would be an industry-specific coach, or maybe a podcast that interviews thought leaders in a particular field. If you get stuck here, just spend a bit of time on social media and see who is trending or posting things that you think would resonate with your ideal client. Once you identify a few people or brands, then start becoming more descriptive of who else might be like those individuals.

Ideally, you have a few very specific people or organizations listed here.

Trust: Who Has An Intimate Relationship With Your Ideal Clients?

This list will likely include a variety of people or organizations that you have already outlined, but it's important to understand which of the people on your list your ideal clients trust. If they have a certain level of trust with a person or organization on your list then their referrals will mean more than that of a general vendor. Trust is usually found where there is a deep relationship. These could be financial advisors, estate attorneys, CPAs, or other advisors who know sensitive information about your clients. These types of relationships typically take longer to develop, but once they're established they are usually not replaced easily.

You may not add any new ideas to this list, you might simply rewrite some of the people or organizations you've already identified. However, you may also find that there are some real opportunities that you haven't considered before.

Connectors: Who Do You Know That Knows Everybody?

Lastly, we have connectors— the individuals who seem to know everybody. You likely can think of a handful of people in your network right now that meet this description. These are the people you reach out to when you need to solve a problem and don't have the right resource in your direct network. Connectors are the most valuable part of any growth strategy as they are a great resource for you, your ideal clients, and your network.

When we get to the "adding value" part of the Connection Expansion System™, Connectors will play a pivotal role in tipping the scale for you.

Ideally, you've identified a few people in your current network that you believe are Connectors. As we talk about the strategies to get this system started, keep these people in mind.

Tying It All Together

At this point you should have a set of lists containing people or organizations that align with one of the sections above: vendors, education, gather, influence, trust, and connection. Hopefully, by this point, you are starting to see how this strategy works. Now I would like you to circle two different types of people or organizations on the list. First, I want you to circle the ones that you think have access to a lot of your ideal clients *and* that your industry is likely overlooking.

Second, I want you to circle the ones where you have a stronger ability to build relationships via your story, your experience, your passions, the way you communicate, etc. What people/organizations will you be the most confident and comfortable having conversations with? If you find that you've circled a person or organization both times then those are likely your highest-value connections.

Now Let's Do The Connection Expansion Exercise™ Again

There are two ways you should go back through the Connection Expansion Exercise™.

The first is to go back through the exercise with a different ideal client in mind. How do your various lists change? Where is there overlap? This might help you identify people or organizations who have access to *all of* your ideal client profiles. If that's the case then they should move up your priority list, as you move through the Connection Expansion System™.

The second way you should go back through the exercise is with one of your highest-value connections in mind. Ideally, this would be a person (or type of person) who has access to a lot of your ideal clients and whom you would be very confident and comfortable talking with. The true power of the many-to-many approach lies in shifting your focus to building your lists around how to reach these individuals.

Let's assume that business CPAs are great potential referral partners for you. Begin by focusing on who has access to business CPAs. You may find associations or accreditations focused strictly on CPAs who work with businesses. You could find business coaches who help CPAs scale their firms or software that business CPAs use that standard CPAs likely don't.

By identifying these individuals or organizations, you create a list for building strategies to become the go-to resource for business CPAs. Now you can put your efforts into positioning yourself in situations where you are in a room full of referral partners. Over time, as you nurture that room, you will scale your pipeline potential exponentially.

> **Schedule Your Personalized Connection Expansion Exercise™ Strategy Session Today!**
>
> The more time and energy you spend gaining confidence and clarity with your outputs from the Connection Expansion Exercise™, the better you will be able to move through the rest of the Connection Expansion System™. You can sign up for a personalized Connection Expansion Exercise™ strategy session, which will give you an outside perspective and direct guidance as you move through the process. Visit www.ConnectionExpansionExercise.com to learn more.

Shifting Your Ask

If I asked you before going through the Connection Expansion Exercise™ who you wanted to be connected with, you, like most others, would have answered with some description of your ideal client and why those would be great connections or why you can provide value to those connections.

Once you've gone through the exercise, hopefully your ask changes to the high-value connection you identified. If you're going to receive 1 - 3 connections from someone, wouldn't you rather they be the highest-value connections that have access to the most amount of your ideal clients? That's much more impactful long-term than hoping you get connected to 1 - 3 ideal clients. Remember, it is much harder to make ideal client connections due to the friction that results from the perception of that contact being "sold" something— even if it is something they need.

Hopefully, once you go through the exercise a second time with your highest-value connection in mind, you shift your ask from connecting to one high-value connection to connecting with people who have access to a lot of high-value connections.

Let's explore a real example so you can apply this concept to the lists you created and the asks you will be using as we move into the next steps of the system.

- **Ideal Client-Focused Ask**: Business owners in the healthcare industry who are doing X revenue per year and have X employees.
- **Adjusted Ask**: Consultants who work with the ideal client outlined above.
- **Further Adjusted Ask**: People who help healthcare consultants to scale their businesses.

In this example, you start by defining an ideal client. That is critical as you definitely do want to be introduced to an ideal client who expresses a need for your product or service. Next, adjust your ask to be connected with people who educate, have influence, and are vendors to your ideal clients. Lastly, shift your ask to connect with thought leaders or consultants who help the consultants your clients seek advice from. In this example, if you could find yourself in a conversation with a consultant who has several clients fitting your highest-value profile, then you have found the goldmine for yourself and your network.

The magic of the Connection Expansion System™ is that it only takes a few high-value connections to unlock the exponential growth power of the system.

In the next chapter, we'll start to explore how you take the information gathered in this chapter and use it to evaluate, and hopefully adjust, how you're currently handling sales, marketing, and new connection development for yourself and your business.

CHAPTER 4

Making New Connections

"Your network is your net worth. How do you value your network? Well, if you don't value it, cultivate it, nurture it, it becomes worthless. If you do value it, it becomes priceless."

— Robert G. Allen

By now I'm hoping you have started to shift your perspective regarding the types of relationships you are asking for and the potential power of building many-to-many relationships. In this chapter, I will walk you through how to carry this change in perspective into your new connection strategies.

Quick Results Exercise & Sample Email Script

For those of you reading this who are eager to start generating results, I wanted to include this section for you. It doesn't take a lot of connections to get the ball rolling. In fact, you could set up meetings with three people in your current network and you'll start to see how the Connection Expansion System™ can start working for you.

That said, I would highly recommend reading the rest of the book before you book those meetings as you have to change the way you are booking and conducting those meetings to get the long-term results the system will generate.

Here is a simple email script you can use to set up those meetings:

Disclaimer: This is the first of many email scripts that will be provided throughout the book. The subjects and scripts have been tested over many years and generate predictable results. Feel free to adjust to fit your personality and messaging style. However, be very careful not to shift the language to be "salesy" or follow best practices for direct-response messaging. You will likely find that you get a lower response rate or negative responses.

Subject: Checking In - How Are You? **OR** Checking In - Let's Get Together

[NAME],

I hope you are doing well and that you are having a great day!

It has been a while since we last connected and I wanted to check in with you to see how you are doing.

Anything new and exciting in your world? Any new challenges?

I would love to set up a time to catch up with you and realign on what types of connections would be best for you.

How does your schedule look for the next couple of weeks?

I look forward to meeting with you!

Have a great day!

[YOUR NAME]

As you move through this chapter please remember the core principles of the Connection Expansion System™:

- Always Add Value
- Control What You Can Control
- There Is Value In Every Relationship
- Never Make Assumptions About A Connection
- You Have To Train By Doing

It is critical that you keep these in mind as you move through the various stages since it can be very easy to slip back into old habits, which may set you up for failure.

Setting Your Intention

As I previously discussed, you must have the right goal when making new connections. You need to make sure that the goal you have is a goal that you can control. My recommendation is to simply have the goal to *meet as many people as possible and get their contact information*. There are countless variables beyond your control in the different environments where you might make new connections, whether in person or virtually, so it's essential to ensure your goal is structured to set you up for success.

Have A Plan For Conversations

Another way you can succeed is to have a clear plan for how you'll engage in conversations. By having a plan, you can approach conversations with confidence, avoid getting stuck in one conversation for the entire event, and prevent others from dominating the discussion. These factors could derail your ability to meet as many people as possible.

If you're intimidated walking into a room full of strangers, having a clear plan for how you'll engage in conversations will set you up for success. If you're already confident in these types of environments, having a plan will hold you accountable to the process and keep you from talking too much!

Here are the exact questions I have used for the last decade that have worked for hundreds of clients:

- What do you do?
- How long have you been doing that?
- Two options based on the previous answer
    - If their answer is less than a year - What did you do before?
    - If their answer is more than a year - You must love what you do!

- Who is an ideal client for you?

Now I will take a second to explain *why* I ask those questions so you can have a deeper understanding.

What Do You Do?

This is pretty straightforward. I need to ideally discover the role, industry, and company of the person I am talking to. This starts to give me an idea of where they might fit into the web of contacts I created during the Connection Expansion Exercise™.

How Long Have You Been Doing That?

I love to ask this question because it lets you know a few things about the person you are talking to. First, if they have been doing something for less than a year, there is more to their story than what they are currently doing. They are also likely still getting settled and may not have as deep of a network or understanding of their industry. They may be on a journey to build credibility and authority in their new role.

Conversely, if they've been doing something for a long time then they likely have deep and well-established relationships inside their industry. They may have some rich customer relationships and are likely an authority in their field. Knowing these things will help us consider the types of connections that might be valuable for the person as we strengthen the relationship.

Two Options Based On Their Previous Answer

Now that the person has given you some information, you need to make a decision on which direction to go with the conversation. If they have been doing whatever they are doing for less than a year I like to ask about what they did before. This helps me start to connect some dots on the potential network they may have from the previous work they were doing and also helps me better understand their journey.

If they've been doing what they're doing for over a year, I like to make a statement like, "You must love what you are doing." I find that people usually answer one of two ways. They may start talking about why they are passionate about what they are doing, which is like winning the lottery for you. You've quickly gotten the person to have a passionate conversation with you, which will create a memorable moment for them. On the other hand, they may say something that feels like a burnout statement and how the industry has worn them down. That is very insightful as well and may speak to challenges they are facing, which may help you make a different set of connections for them as you deepen the relationship.

Who Is Your Ideal Client?

This one seems straightforward but is a critical question to ask. It tells you how clear the person is on their ideal client and their ask. It also helps you understand the many-to-many relationships that you could connect them with access to their ideal client.

Rules For Engagement

Above, I've shared the questions I ask with a bit of my reasoning. Now I want to share some rules for engagement that will help you have more success as you're making new connections.

First, *always control the conversation*. You should ask all four questions before the other person asks you questions about yourself. This is part of the "control what you can control" mentality. You have to learn about the person you're talking to so you set yourself up for success. If the other person asks you a question first, answer quickly and then start down your series of questions. This also ties into the fourth point below, allowing you to respond to any questions they ask with answers that align with what you just learned about the person you're talking to.

Second, *when you ask who their ideal client is, ask them for a business card at that moment* and take a quick note on the back of the business card with information about their ideal client.

Third, *get out of the conversation*. When you're at a networking event, your goal is to connect with as many people as possible. Don't let the conversation go too long. Have an exit strategy so you can gracefully exit the conversation and start a new conversation. You can use food, drink, or the bathroom as an excuse if you really feel stuck. I usually just say something like, "It was great meeting you, best of luck on your networking tonight."

Another great option when it comes to exiting a conversation is to connect the person you are talking with to someone you just met: "I just met _____ and based on our conversation, I think you two should connect". Then you can walk over to the other person, make a quick introduction, and excuse yourself so that they can meet each other. This is a great way to add value while exiting the conversation.

Fourth, *what you do, others will likely do too*. Most people are not actually comfortable in a networking environment. If you control the conversation, you will help them build up their confidence and have a positive experience. In addition, there is a high probability that they will ask you the exact same questions you just asked them. This is a form of mirroring and sets you up for success. If you can answer the four questions you are asking of others, there is a high probability that you will have a very successful event.

Always Do A Retrospective

After every event I highly recommend that you take 15 minutes to jot down some notes about what went well and what you feel you didn't do well. If you didn't leave the event with contact information for any new connections, then really explore why. The event may have been the wrong type of event for you, or maybe you slipped back into trying to find clients in a room full of connection opportunities. Make sure you're real with yourself at this moment and reflect on what you could've done better to meet more people and get their contact information. This will help set you up for success as you head into the next event.

High-Value Connections At A Birthday Party

Before we move on to what to do with the new connections you've made, I wanted to share a story with you about a birthday party I attended a few years ago. This was a birthday party for a 4-year-old classmate from my daughter's preschool. As you can imagine, it involved the kids running around and playing, while the parents stood awkwardly around trying to have small talk with the other parents. Many of us parents didn't know each other well, only seeing each other briefly at drop off or pick up. Now I happen to love being in these situations as it's like a game for me. Using what I know about relationships, I know there is value in getting to know the other parents.

I started working my way around the room and used my set of questions to learn more about each parent. After a few conversations, I found myself in a conversation with a gentleman whose parents owned a business and had a need for what I do. In addition, he mentioned that his wife was in charge of scheduling speakers for an association she was part of. This one conversation had opened the door to a potential client and a potential speaking engagement. I did end up having some other great conversations and getting contact information for many of the parents, but this particular conversation would turn out to be very valuable over time.

After the party, I followed up, as outlined in the coming chapters, and moved the person I talked with, his parents, and his wife through the process. A couple of years later, I've done business with the man's parents and have spoken at three events that his wife was in charge of coordinating, resulting in dozens of new connections.

All of this started through a conversation at a birthday party. I could share countless stories of similar conversations at coffee shops, the grocery store, random get-togethers, and more. Whether you're an extrovert or introvert, having a clear plan for building confidence in conversations will empower you to uncover the hidden value in every situation.

In the callout at the beginning of the chapter, I shared one sample email script for how to book meetings with people you already know. In the next chapter, I will share with you the timing, email scripts, and best practices for following up with any new connection you make.

CHAPTER 5

Booking Connection Meetings

"48% of sales people never follow up with a prospect.
25% of sales people make a second contact and stop.
12% of sales people only make three contacts and stop."

— Stats from the National Sales Executive Association

This chapter walks you through what to do once you have made a new connection— whether from an event, tradeshow, another person, or any other opportunity that landed you with someone else's contact information.

Realigning Your Goal

Before we can jump into the "how" I need to make sure you have the right goal as you move into the follow-up and meeting process. Your goal when you are following up is to set up a Connection Meeting. This is a meeting that should have no agenda (there is one, but it's not about selling) and should be focused on you learning about the other person.

This is where I see a lot of people revert to old habits. You may slip some "sales" language into your follow-up emails, you may dig too deep too quickly during the meeting, or you may want to talk about yourself. All of these things are great if the person you're meeting expresses a clear need for the services you sell.

In that case, by all means, move them into your sales process and follow whatever best practices you have there. However, for everybody else who hasn't expressed a direct interest in doing business with you, don't slip into those habits! You must trust the process as every step of the process builds upon the previous to create the desired outcome you're looking for.

Timing Matters, But Is Not Everything

The best rule of thumb is that you should follow up with a new connection within 24 hours of making the connection or receiving an introduction. That said, don't beat yourself up if you're a bit delayed in starting the follow-up process. I've had just as much success with a delayed follow-up, but I have to be intentional about making time to move the connections through the process.

In Chapter 9, I'll talk to you about contact and task management. As you dive deeper into this process, it will be critical to have a system in place that holds you accountable to the process and doesn't let anyone slip through the cracks.

Following Up Is Where You Win

I am not going to quote a bunch of sales statistics about the number of touches you have to close a deal, or the fact that most salespeople fail in the follow-up. I simply want you to know that if you have a process in place for following up, you will set yourself apart from the majority of people trying to build a network.

Think about where you might have a pile of business cards that you've done nothing with. This is very normal. In the virtual world, this may be a contact list that you never take action on.

By the time you are done with this book, you'll see how you can throw away all of those business cards and ensure that you are taking action on every contact you meet.

Control What You Can Control

Yes, we are back to this topic again. As we move into the follow-up process, it's critical that you "control what you can control". You can control the frequency and timing of your follow-up. You can also control the messaging you use so you set yourself up for success. If you control these things, you'll find that your calendar will fill up more than it ever has before.

The Follow Up For Success Process

Now, let's talk about the recommended process for following up with new connections. Please stick with me during this section. I'm Sure you're going to say something like, "This feels like too much" or "Won't I be too pushy or annoying?" The answer is *no*. I'll share the exact messaging you'll use in the next section. If you use this messaging and don't slip into old habits, this process will work almost every time!

I recommend that you send the first message (usually an email) within 24 hours of making a new connection. This means that if you're going to go to a networking event, then you should buffer time on your calendar the next day to do the follow-up from the event.

After the first touch, you should follow up every three business days for five additional times. After those six touches (the first one and the additional five), follow up once a week for four more touches. After those ten touches, you can then move the contact into the nurture process, which I'll explain in Chapter 8.

I strictly use email for my follow-up touches. You may find that you prefer phone calls. If that is the case, I recommend you rotate between email and phone calls every other touch. Also, if you make a phone call, always leave a voicemail and send a follow-up email after you leave a voicemail.

Some tips for success:

- You may experience a higher response rate by replying to a previously sent email.
- You may have a higher book rate if you include a link to book a meeting rather than waiting for a link or trading emails to lock down a time.

The Scripts For Following Up

The language you use when scheduling a first meeting is critical. Below I will share a few different email scripts with you based on how you made or received the connection.

Here is the standard email template for following up from an event to schedule a Connection Meeting:

Subject: Great Meeting You - Let's Get Together

> ***Hi [insert name here],***
>
> ***I hope you are doing well and that you are having a great day!***
>
> ***It was great meeting you at the [insert event name] with the [insert event organization].***
>
> ***I enjoyed briefly learning about you and your business (or what you do). I would love to set up a time to learn more about you and your business so that I can better refer people to you.***
>
> ***How does your schedule look for the next couple of weeks? (or insert a link to your calendar)***
>
> ***I look forward to meeting with you!***
>
> ***Have a great day!***

Here is the email template I use to reply to a previously sent email.

> ***Hi [insert name here],***
>
> ***I hope you are doing well and that you are having a great day!***
>
> ***I wanted to bump the below email.***
>
> ***I would love to set up a time to learn more about you and your business.***
>
> ***How does your schedule look for the next couple of weeks? (or insert a link to your calendar)***
>
> ***I look forward to meeting with you!***
>
> ***Have a great day!***

Here is the voicemail script I use when adding phone calls to the process.

> ***Hi [insert name here],***
>
> ***I hope you are doing well and that you are having a great day!***
>
> ***It was great meeting you at the [insert event name] with the [insert event organization].***

I enjoyed briefly learning about you and your business (or what you do).

I have sent a few emails and I haven't heard back from you.

I would love to set up a time to learn more about you and your business.

How does your schedule look for the next couple of weeks?

Feel free to give me a call back or I will send you an email following this voicemail that will have a link to my calendar if that is more convenient for you.

I look forward to meeting with you!

Have a great day!

Here is the email script I use when following up with a connection I was directly connected to.

Hi [insert name here],

I hope you are doing well and that you are having a great day!

It is great to virtually meet you via [insert name here]'s introduction.

I would love to set up a time to learn more about you and your business.

How does your schedule look for the next couple of weeks? (or insert a link to your calendar)

I look forward to meeting with you!

Have a great day!

You can download these scripts and other resources related to strategies talked about in this book at www.ConnectionExpansionBook.com

What you should notice by now is that 100% of the follow-up touches are about the other person, the value you can bring to the other person, and use assumptive language about getting together.

If you use the above scripting you'll find that you book more meetings. There's no friction to book a meeting with you and the people you are following up with should not feel like they are booking a meeting to be "sold" by you.

What Happens When You Get A Negative Response?

No process is perfect. Although this should be a very small percentage of the people you're following up with, you will get a few versions of a "negative response."

One version is someone directly saying, "Please stop following up with me." I usually reply to them with, "No worries. I thought we had a great conversation and I was excited to learn more about you and see what connections I could make for you. I will go ahead and remove you from my follow-up list." Then I usually shift them to the nurture process, which we will cover in Chapter 8.

Another version is someone saying, "Why do you want to get together?" (or some version of that). I usually just reinforce my messaging: "I want to learn more about you and what you do so that I can make some connections for you if I come across anybody who might be a fit." Sometimes they will push back and ask about your motive or push harder. I simply restate the same things I have already said. You have to realize that many of the people you will be following up with are stuck in the always-hunting clients mindset. If you don't fit into what they perceive as a potential client, they may not book a meeting. That's fine, just keep them in the process until you shift them to the nurture process.

Remember, there is value in every relationship. You have to buy into this belief 100% for the system to work. You will find that many people you follow up with don't have that belief and it's your job to make sure they see value and get value in connecting with you!

Now at some point in the process, the majority of people you are following up with will book a meeting with you. If you are meeting in person, these meetings are usually an hour long. If you are meeting virtually, these meetings tend to be 20 - 30 minutes. The length of the meeting is not really what is important. How you navigate the meeting is the secret to determining what defines a successful Connection Meeting, which is exactly what I will cover in the next chapter.

CHAPTER 6

Having A Successful Connection Meeting

"Most people think 'selling' is the same as 'talking.' But the most effective salespeople know that listening is the most important part of their job."

— Roy Bartell

Congratulations, you have a meeting (or hopefully multiple meetings) booked. Now, how should these meetings be conducted so that you stay true to all the messaging you've been using throughout the process?

I could fill a whole book with tips and strategies on how to do consultative sales, and why you need to properly align your value with the client's needs, but that is not the focus of this book. The focus is to help you build deeper relationships that will open doors for you to high-value, many-to-many relationships, thus unlocking the full potential of your network.

Whether you booked this meeting following a networking event, a direct introduction, or as a catch-up meeting with someone you know, I recommend that you follow a very similar format as you move through the meeting.

Have A Plan And Follow The Plan

As with networking, your approach to Connection Meetings requires a clear plan and you need to strive to keep the meeting inside of the plan. As stated in the last chapter, the amount of time for these meetings is not really critical although anything longer than an hour is probably too much.

What Are Your Goals For The Meeting?

You need to have the right goals as you head into a Connection Meeting. Again, I warn you not to slip back into the habit of selling. Your goals need to be things you can control and are designed to set you up for long-term success with the person you are meeting with.

Here are the goals that I recommend:

- You need to learn enough about the person to make high-impact connections to them. Ideally, you have three connections clearly identified before the end of the meeting.
- You need to learn enough about the person to understand what types of high-value connections they can potentially make for you.
- You need to learn enough about the person that when you make connections you can properly explain what the person does and edify them to the person you are

connecting them to. *This goal is critical when you move into the next chapter which will walk you through the follow-up process after a meeting.*

If you accomplish the above goals during a Connection Meeting, you are setting the relationship up for great long-term success.

The Meeting Flow

As stated above, I recommend you have a plan for the meeting. That includes the above goals and a clear flow of conversation that you move the person through.

As with networking, you should control the conversation, which allows you to ask questions and for the other person to talk. If you find yourself talking too much in a Connection Meeting, you are going to find it hard to hit the goals that are defined above. You should approach these meetings as if you are a journalist and are trying to craft a story about the person you are meeting with. You need to be an avid notetaker as you move through the process. This will help you keep track of the action items you'll take and the connections you'll make and also tell the person that you are actively and deeply listening to them.

Here is how I recommend you structure your conversation.

First, start with a conversation about the *"current state"*. What does the person do? Who do they serve? What are their core services? What are the services that people may not know they offer? What services are they most excited about? What is going on in their industry that is exciting, challenging, or changing? Focus on questions like this.

Second, move the conversation into an exploration of *"how they got here"*. There is so much you can learn about a person when you dive into their backstory and explore why and how they got to where they are today.

Third, make the big jump to the *"desired future state"*. Once you feel like you have a better understanding of the person's story, shift the conversation to the goals and dreams. What are the goals for their business or themselves? What do they want to accomplish in the short-term and long-term? What are the big goals that they don't really talk about? Do they have any personal goals that are fueled by their professional success? Focus on future-looking questions and make sure you take the time needed to allow them to share their vision and dreams with you.

Fourth, ask them about *"challenges and roadblocks"*. At this point, you should understand their current state and their desired future state. You should now take time to explore what is in the way of their desired future state. I usually transition to this by saying, "Thank you for sharing your vision with me, I love it! What is in the way of you achieving that?". Give them time to talk through this part of the conversation. This is where you should be able to start identifying connections that can move the needle for this person or you may see where your product or service could be valuable to them.

At this point, you should have everything you need to align with the above-mentioned goals. There is usually a natural pause somewhere during the last part of the conversation and the other person will say something like, "Oh my gosh, we are running out of time, tell me about you!". If you've done the above steps correctly you should only have 15 - 20% of the meeting time left to talk about yourself and answer any questions they may ask you.

What you'll find is they'll often follow a similar flow to what you just walked them through, just in a much quicker manner due to the time constraints of the meeting—which is perfect!

As you are answering their questions, be concise and intentional. Answer in a way that shows you are someone who can help solve their problems and add value to them, not just through your product or service, but through key connections you can make for them. Help them see the value you bring to the table.

As you wrap up the meeting, always let them know what actions you'll take. Let them know you will be making connections for them, sending them information that you identified, or sending them information about your product or service (if they asked for it).

The Power Of A Book As A Leave Behind

If you are an author, as part of your Connection Meeting it is very powerful to bring a copy of your book for the person you're meeting with. You can sign the book for them ahead of time and maybe even include a nice bookmark.

In addition, you would give them a second copy so that they can share it with someone else. This positions you as an authority and gives the person you are meeting with the ability to add value to someone else following your meeting.

If you're meeting virtually you could send a book ahead of time or at the end of the meeting. Simply ask for their address and let them know you'll be sending them a package with a copy of your book.

Books have a tangible value, so when they get that package in the mail you are providing direct value to that connection.

If you haven't yet written a book, it doesn't have to be a long and stressful process. Reach out to my friends at Million Dollar Author to learn how they can help you write a book that will solidify your authority while adding more value to those who receive the book.

Visit www.DevinSizemore.com/MDA to learn more.

If the person you are talking to is open to adding value, they will often ask who a great connection would be for you. This is where you need to answer with the highest-value relationship you identified during the Connection Expansion Exercise™ in Chapter 3. The difference here is that you should also answer with a connection type that you believe they have access to, based on everything you've learned about that person.

Don't try to do too much in these meetings. Just follow the above flow with the few goals that are outlined and make sure you approach the meeting with a genuine curiosity about the person you are meeting with. You should find through the conversation that there really is value in every relationship.

In the next chapter, we'll talk about the actions to take following a Connection Meeting. These action items will be a key moment in the process and determine the overall success.

CHAPTER 7

Connection Meeting Follow-Up

"Little did I realize that my desire to add value to others would be the thing that added value to me."

— John C. Maxwell

Again, I want to congratulate you for making it this far in the process. Great job sticking to the plan, not jumping into "sales mode", and actually taking an approach where you are curious and demonstrate that you care about others.

Your follow-up after a Connection Meeting will set the foundation for success and determine the value you can gain from the person you just met.

Do What You Said You Would Do

At the end of your meeting you should have made it clear what action you'll be taking after. Ideally, you should have three connections in mind for the person you met and identified any other value-driven action you said you were going to take. Now the key to making this all work is simple: do what you said you were going to do! It sounds basic, but you would be amazed how often I meet with someone who claims they will make introductions or take some sort of action and never follow up after the meeting. Remember, most people default to "sales mode" and if you are not an ideal client interested in buying their product or service, they will not prioritize following up with you.

Now is your chance to do what you said, which in turn will teach that person how to properly add value following a meeting.

The first thing you should do is send a follow-up email within 24 hours of the meeting. In this email, express that you enjoyed the meeting, confirm any action items you will be taking, and summarize any action items they mentioned they would take. If you identified any resources that would be beneficial or they expressed interest in getting more information about your product or service, include that information in your follow-up email as well.

Make Connections

Next, you need to send out the three connection emails. You should have identified these three people during the meeting and now you need to connect the person with them. I highly recommend that you make these connections via email unless the person you are connecting with will only respond via text or on some social media messaging platform. I have a much higher follow-through rate when I make or receive connections via email.

When you are crafting the introduction email I recommend you follow the format below.

In the subject line put "Introduction - [Name] and [Name]." This makes it very clear that you are connecting one person with the other and also helps keep the email conversations you are sending separate. Sometimes I may add in a reason for the introduction in the subject line, but not often.

In the body of the email, write a direct message to each person. I usually start with the person I didn't meet with. This lets that person know quickly who you are connecting them with and why. When you are introducing one person to another make sure you clearly state what they do, you edify their expertise in some way shape, or form, and then you include a sentence or two on why you think the two parties should connect.

Next, you write a direct message to the person you met about the person you are connecting them with following the same format as above.

I usually sign off with a sentence that says something like, "I am sure you both will find value in this connection." I always want to set the expectation that there is value in the two people connecting.

Educating Through The Process

During the process of making connections, especially to people who are new to your approach to networking there may be some pushback or disconnect. I find that this is a small percentage of people you'll be connecting, but it is worth discussing as it will happen.

You may get people who are connected and ask you why they were connected or let you know that they don't want any more connections. I recommend starting by clearly explaining to that person the value you see in them meeting the people you connected them with. For example, you may say, "I connected you with Joe as I found out he has access to a few coaches that I believe to be your target market. I think Joe could open some very strategic doors for you." Most of the time, the person asking for clarification will understand and move forward with taking the meeting. Sometimes, they may push back and still say they don't see value in the connection as it is not a potential client. In this case, no worries, simply remove the person from your future connection list and move on.

Permission To Follow Up

Here is where the process gets really fun. By making aligned, edified connections, you've earned permission to follow up with both parties. I highly recommend you give yourself a note (or task) to follow up with both parties individually three weeks after the initial connection.

I like to check in on the person who received the three connections to see if they were able to book meetings and how those meetings went. The majority of the time the feedback will be positive. On rare occasions, you may receive some negative feedback about a person or a conversation. Make sure you note this because any "takers" that you connect people to will tarnish your reputation and mess up your value proposition.

For the person you connected to, I like to send a simple check-in email and if you'd like to meet with them, now is a great time to suggest getting together to catch up.

Playing The Long Game

Once you've sent your check-in email to both parties, I recommend that you move all parties into a nurture process, which we will discuss in the next chapter. You may not get any connections in return from the person you met with, and that is okay. They may not follow up with you on the actions they said they would take, and that is also okay.

You can't control the other person or what they do. You *can* control how you follow up and show them that you are committed to adding value to them and the other people in your network. This will create "value equity" or an imbalance of the value provided versus the value received. As long as you are providing more value to your network, the system will work for you in the long run.

What If You Can't Think Of Any Connections?

When you're getting started, you may find it hard for you to make connections with the people you are meeting with. That is natural and is something you will become much more proficient with over time.

The easiest answer is to connect them with a Connector. A Connector should be your default failsafe should you not have a clear connection in mind. There is a very high likelihood that a

Connector will open some high-value doors for the person you connect them with and, in turn, will make you look great.

Another way that I like to think about the types of connections you're making is to do a brief Connection Expansion Exercise™ for the person you met with. You aren't actually doing the exercise with them, but you can go through the thought process based on the ideal client profile they told you and find some hidden value in your network for that person.

You are most likely not going to be introducing them to an ideal client unless you happen to come across someone who expresses a clear need for their product or service. In that case, by all means, make an introduction as fast as possible!

In the next chapter, I will walk you through the nurture process, which is where all of the people in your network should end up at some point.

CHAPTER 8

Long-term Connection Nurturing

"Building and repairing relationships are long-term investments."

— Stephen Covey

To start this chapter I want to make a statement that might make you uncomfortable or that you might even disagree with—and I am okay with that.

Every single contact in your network should be part of the nurture process.

Why would you put the time and energy into making connections—whether in person or via social media—if you're not going to take action on those connections? If you've had a conversation with someone, and they have given you their contact information, then you must nurture those contacts forever.

The process discussed in this chapter doesn't work with cold leads. The nurture process is for people who are in your network, know who you are, and have had a conversation with you at some point. They've given their contact information to you, now it's up to you to maintain and grow that connection.

You'll find much more success in this process if you have a clear system for managing contacts and tasks, which we will discuss in the next chapter. I want to note that here because many people like to tap out at this point for fear of it becoming "too much".

Your Message Matters

Let's start by restating what has been said throughout the previous chapters. The message you use when nurturing your network is critical to the long-term success that we are trying to create. You cannot slip back into sales mode at any point during the process. I will share a couple of scripts with you later in the chapter that you can use to help open the door for potential sales while keeping your message aligned with the nurturing process.

If you become too salesy at any point, your network will tune you out, and they won't respond the way you would like them to in the long-term.

Overview Of The Process

Let's talk about how people enter your nurture process.

First, anyone who's gone through the initial touchpoints but hasn't booked a Connection Meeting should enter the process. Next, anyone you've met with in a Connection Meeting is automatically a part of the process. Lastly, anyone who is in your network that is not a "cold contact" should be included.

In the nurture process, you will keep it very simple. You will be sending a check-in email every 30, 45, 60, or 90 days depending on the perceived value of the connection. I recommend that you rate your connections on a scale from HOT to COOL (but not cold).

A "hot" contact is a high-value connection—someone that you get a lot of referrals from or an important person in your network. This also includes anyone you recently met and are still feeling out for long-term value. I would recommend sending these contacts a check-in email every 30 or 45 days. Personally, I like the 45-day check-in, but sometimes 30 days is ideal for staying top of mind.

A "warm" contact is someone to whom you've added value, or they've added value to you. These contacts hold potential, but you haven't had a recent meeting or received recent value. These contacts should receive a check-in email every 60 days.

Lastly, any "cool" contacts should receive a check-in email from you every 90 days. These are all the other contacts in your network that fit the above criteria and aren't "cold" leads.

Scripts For Nurturing

Let's start with the standard script that I recommend you use. I've used this script for over a decade and so have many of my clients. You will likely see a 15 - 25% response rate depending on the value you have created with the contacts in your network.

Here is the recommended check-in email script:

> **Subject:** Checking In - How Are You?
>
> I hope you are doing well and that you are having a great day!
>
> It has been awhile since we last connected and I wanted to check in with you to see how you are doing.
>
> Anything new and exciting? Any big wins? Any new challenges?
>
> Let me know if there are any connections I can make for you.
>
> I look forward to hearing back from you.
>
> Have a great day!

That's it.

That's the whole script. It doesn't have to be more complicated than that. Your goal with check-in emails is to stay top of mind with your network and to keep the door open for communication.

Now, if you want to fill your calendar, replace the "I look forward to hearing back from you" line with something like: "I would love to set up a time to catch up with you. How does your schedule look for the next few weeks? I look forward to meeting with you".

You can reference back to the script that was provided at the beginning of Chapter 4. This is a great way to get people back on your calendar, realign with them, add more value to them, and gain permission to follow up with them and the people you connect them with after the catch-up meeting.

Now, I do sometimes add some "asks" into my check-in emails. This is done intentionally and should not be used all of the time. For example, I might clearly ask for a specific type of connection I'm looking for. I might say something like "I have had some great conversations with [insert connection type] recently and would love to connect with more people like that if there is anyone in your network that comes to mind."

What About Being Annoying?

The real success of the nurture process is that you continue to send check-in emails forever. Or at least until people tell you to stop reaching out to them. Of the thousands of connections I've made over the years, only a handful of people have drawn this type of line. That's great—I don't and you don't need people like that in your network anyways.

Some people may reply and say, "Why do you keep sending these automated emails?" or "I have received this same email from you multiple times," or some version of that. When I receive these responses I use a canned reply that sounds like this:

> *It is great to hear from you! That is why I send out these emails. It is always nice to catch up and see what is new with you and others in my network. It helps me*

find ways to add value to you and others in my network and also keeps me informed of any pivots you have made. With that said, how are you? What is new that I should know about?

When they reply with anything other than "stop", the email did its job. It opened up a conversation between you and someone in your network. I have been sending out these emails for so long to so many people that there are definitely people in my network who have received this email more than a hundred times.

What About Newsletters And Automation?

Here is where I get the most pushback, so let's take a moment to talk about these two topics.

First, a newsletter is not the same as a plain text email sent out from your email platform. A newsletter can serve a lot of purposes, but at the core, it is assumed to be a mass email sent to several people in your database.

Second, automation of a plain text email is not recommended either. There are plenty of tools that can do this for you and do it well. However, this automation doesn't take into account any recent connections you may have made to the contact or the fact that you have recently run into them and caught up briefly. If you have done any of these things and they receive a check-in email, it becomes very clear that you are automating the process which takes away the perceived value of the check-ins you are making.

I highly recommend that you personally send an email to each contact when their check-in task or note pops up on your to-do list. I use a shortcode tool that populates the check-in email, but you can just as easily copy and paste the email. You can send a check-in email every 30 seconds, which includes the time to schedule or put a note for when you should send the next one. This means that in 10 minutes you should be able to check-in with 20 people or so. Depending on the size of your network, this is probably an ample amount of time as that means that you will be reaching out to 100 people per week or more than 5,000 people per year. That is likely more contacts than most of the people reading this book should be sending check-in emails to. Remember, this is not your cold list.

Best Practices For Nurturing

Many of the best practices for nurturing are built into the timing and messaging process that I've just shared. But I wanted to share a few others with you.

First, anytime you talk with someone or see someone, make sure you adjust your check-in to be at the right cadence based on the level of the contact. This goes for anyone who replies to one of your check-in emails as well. Make sure to adjust your follow-up based on the last touch you had with them, spacing it out by an appropriate amount of time. This will make sure you aren't checking in too often with a singular contact.

Second, don't be afraid to show some love. There is a lot of value in a handwritten card, a small gift, a copy of your book, or a copy of another book that could be valuable to them. These high-impact touches can be a great way to check-in with your network and fall in line with your already established cadence.

Third, have fun. This process should not feel like a burden. Nurturing your network is critical for creating long-term value and generating referrals. Have fun with it and use the nurturing time to actually think about the people you're reaching out to as well as any recent new connections that might be a fit for them. What a great way to add more value, get them back toward the top of your network, and set yourself up for more success.

Lastly, track what works. You don't have to be super granular, but make sure you're paying attention to what works. If you adjust the scripts to fit your personality and you seem to be getting a better response rate with a different subject line or sentence in the email, then note that and adjust your future nurturing touches based on what you are seeing is working.

Each of the steps in the Connection Expansion System™ can have a positive impact. When you combine them all together you should see an exponential increase in the connections you receive from your network.

In the next chapter, I will talk through some best practices for task and contact management. Although not required to have success with the system, these processes will help you hold yourself accountable to the process.

CHAPTER 9

Contact & Task Management

"Productivity is never an accident. It is always the result of a commitment to excellence, intelligent planning, and focused effort."

— Paul J. Meyer

Although you can have success with the Connection Expansion System™ without a CRM (contact relationship management) or task management software, you will have a lot more success by putting such a system in place. Not only do these systems keep you organized, but they help free up mental bandwidth. Once you've assigned a task, you don't have to worry about forgetting to take action along the way.

Choosing The Right System

The best part about the Connection Expansion System™ is that you don't need a complex CRM to maximize the system. The CRM you choose only needs to do two things. First, you need to be able to add basic contact information: name, title, company, phone, and email. Second, you need the ability to assign each contact a dated task or "to-do". If the CRM you choose can do those two things, then go for it. There are plenty of great free options out there, choose the one that you think will be best for you.

An additional feature that I find helpful in a CRM is the ability to connect one contact to another contact. This allows me to track who I connect to and who refers someone to me. This can help you understand the overall value you're providing to a specific contact in your network.

Another useful feature is the ability to attach notes or documents directly to a contact. I love keeping my notes from meetings directly linked to each contact. This makes it easier to reference previous conversations and quickly refresh your memory if it's been a while since you last connected.

Contact Management Tips & Tricks

I'd like to provide a few tips and tricks for managing contacts and tasks that may help you streamline your process and get more out of what you're doing. This is not an exhaustive list, just a few things that I think might be valuable.

First, set a rule that every single contact you make must be put into your CRM. Get rid of all the dead piles of business cards or outdated contact lists you have lying around. Put all the information into your CRM and use that as your master database for nurturing your network.

Second, connect with anyone you add to your CRM on the social platforms you are actively using. At a minimum, connect with everyone on LinkedIn. This gives you deeper insight into your contacts' personal and professional lives and keeps you updated on what's happening in their network. As a bonus, make sure to like or follow their business accounts. I promise that they'll notice and it's a small way to add value and show you care.

Lastly, use tags in your CRM if possible. As your network grows, being able to quickly filter and find specific contact types is very helpful. This is also a great way to find possible connections for someone you just met. While there are likely more best practices out there, create a system that allows you to sort your database in a way that works for you.

Task Management Tips & Tricks

First, establish a uniform task-titling structure. I recommend something like "TO DO _ [Action Item]". You can then switch out the "TO DO" with "Email", "Call", "Meeting", "LinkedIn", or some other key action you need to take. You can use the second half to quickly describe the action itself. I find that this formatting allows you to quickly view your tasks by type and easily sort through what action needs to be taken.

Second, make it a rule that every contact in your CRM (except cold contacts) has an assigned task. If you've fully bought into the system, you'll see the value of assigning a nurturing task to each contact.

Third, if you set a meeting with a contact then make sure you assign a task to follow up the next day. You *must follow* up on the action items you said you were going to follow up on. This system doesn't work unless you are driving it.

Fourth, give yourself a buffer time once or twice a week. You are busy, and some things will take priority over managing your contacts. That's fine, but make sure to give yourself time throughout the week to catch up on any action items or follow-ups that you missed.

Let The Process Drive Your CRM And Task Management

When you're choosing a CRM or task management software to support you with this system or any other strategy, make sure that the CRM supports the process and not the other way around. The Connection Expansion System™ works if you work it. Don't try and force the system to fit into whichever CRM you choose. Make sure that the tools you choose support the systems. This same message goes for those of you who are trying to support your sales teams or project management teams. You will find a lot of friction and disappointment if you try to force your processes and systems to fit into the box that a tool gives you.

Keep It Simple

Okay fine, add the other "S": Keep It Simple Stupid (KISS). The strategies outlined in this chapter should not require an exhaustive setup or feel like a burden. Keep it simple and work the process. You will get results by working the system, not spending a ton of time building out your CRM. As noted in the previous chapter, automation is not recommended for this system. While automation has its benefits in other areas of your business, it should not be applied to this process.

Although you can have success with the most basic of tracking systems, having a well-tuned CRM and task management setup will make it easier to scale the system. This will set you up to tap into the full potential of your network.

CHAPTER 10

Unlocking The Untapped Potential In Your Network

"Many of life's failures are people who did not realize how close they were to success when they gave up."

— Thomas Edison

By now I hope you see how the Connection Expansion System™ is a complete and duplicatable system that goes far beyond most (if not all) referral strategies you might find. I am excited for you to start building a high-value network that generates consistent high-value connections and produces predictable referrals for you and your business.

In this chapter, I want to offer you tips on how to get started using resources you likely already have, as well as share some real—and sometimes "hard to believe"—stories about how the Connection Expansion System™ has produced remarkable results for both myself and others.

Using What You Already Have

In Chapter 4, I briefly mentioned reaching out to your existing network to check in and set up meetings. I highly recommend that you do a few more things to get the process moving rapidly.

First, take every business card you have lying around and put them into your CRM. As you are doing this, make sure to connect with those contacts on social media. Then, send a general check-in email - see the previously provided template. I recommend using the template that suggests a meeting as meetings are the place where you have the most control of the process and the ability to really dig for gold in your network.

You can then schedule a nurture task for each contact in 30, 45, 60, or 90 days, depending on the perceived value of the relationship. Set a daily goal for processing these contacts and work through the pile until there are no business cards left. Each contact should take only three to five minutes, so this should not feel overwhelming.

Second, set a goal for the number of people in your database you want to start nurturing and follow the exact same process mentioned above. Reach out to your set number per day, send them a check-in email with a suggestion to book a meeting, and assign nurture tasks based on the perceived value of the relationship. To start, pick the contacts you believe hold the most value and work your way through everyone else. Avoid any cold contacts at this point.

If you complete the two action items mentioned above starting tomorrow, you will begin to fuel the system in a way that will create lasting results. Remember, the system works best with time and volume and these steps will help you accelerate both.

Becoming A Connector For Your Network

Through the Connection Expansion System™ you should find yourself becoming the Connector for your network. When others see you as a Connector, they will see you as a valuable resource, even when they aren't sure how you can help. They'll know that you likely have access to the connection or resource they need.

A great way to position yourself as a Connector is to be on the lookout for ISO (In Search Of) posts on various social media platforms. As you expand your network, you'll find more opportunities to tag others in your network in these posts. While this may not be as impactful as making direct introductions, it's another way to show your network that you are focused on adding value to your connections.

This Book Is A Result Of The System

The very book you are reading is a result of the system that I've outlined. By following the system, I was referred to someone, who then referred me to someone else, who then introduced me to Steve Gordon at Million Dollar Author. Steve and I had a great Connection Meeting and I made several high-value connections for him following our meeting. I then put Steve into a nurture process, which ultimately led to me becoming a client of Million Dollar Author and also a contractor for the company.

The opportunity to write and publish a book, along with a strong contractor partnership, came from trusting the process and being open to new possibilities.

A Friendship Built On The Foundation Of The System

In 2013, I spoke at a networking educational event at a local church. My presentation was on how to build a high-value network. It had pieces of what's discussed in this book, but it wasn't as refined at the time. In the room was a gentleman who was transitioning from the coin/gold industry into the world of health insurance sales. We had a brief conversation at the event, which then led to us having a Connection Meeting.

After our meeting, I followed the process by offering as much value as possible and introduced him to several high-value connections. More than a decade later, I now consider this person a close, trusted friend. Yes, we have made countless connections for each other over the years, but the real value is having a highly trusted friend that's in my inner circle. This relationship began with an invitation to speak at an event and grew from following the system outlined in this book.

Outlasting The Competition

A common theme in many of my client relationships is the ability to outlast the competition through consistent follow-up and nurturing. I can't pinpoint exactly how many times this has happened, but it's fair to say a lot. In one recent example, I was connected to a prospect through a long-term client and referral partner. I had a great first meeting, sent a proposal, and followed up with the prospect. However, it became clear that the prospect wasn't ready to move forward at that time.

I used the system to continue to follow up and nurture the relationship. Around four months later, the prospect called me and said they made a mistake and would like to schedule a meeting. It turned out that the prospect went with a different vendor and wasn't happy with the results they were getting. Because I continued to follow up and nurture the relationship, without being pushy, I was in a position to step in to clean up the mess and solve the prospect's problem when they reached out. I have personally landed seven figures in deals by following this process in this exact way and I would bet that others using the process have landed much more than that in closed deals based on the success stories I have heard.

Finding A Niche Inside A Competitive Industry

I have worked with a lot of professional salespeople over the years, but one realtor stands out. At the time, he was younger and new to the industry, but eager to learn. The office manager at his brokerage connected us and he soon became a client. I introduced him to and helped him implement the Connection Expansion System™. Since then, he has consistently ranked as a top producer at his firm, but the real magic is in how he's done it.

We identified unique relationships where his passions aligned with those of his clients, allowing him to focus his efforts on connecting with those types of people. As a result, he now has a very unique network that fills a very unique need and keeps him out of the "competitive" landscape that many realtors find themselves in. His ability to make specific, high-value asks has built a network that not only benefits his business but continues to grow organically with people others in the industry are not looking or asking for.

Becoming A Sales Leader Among Sales Leaders

I was at a networking event in 2013 and I met a sales leader of a local professional sports team. Over time he moved on to become the president of that organization. I worked with him and the sales team to shift the way they do sales from a high-pressure cold outreach approach to the Connection Expansion System™. Everyone on the team who leaned into the process began seeing new opportunities that had previously been missing.

Years later, this same individual has become the business development manager for a PGA Tour event and also serves on a national sales council where he mentors and teaches best practices to others in the industry. At the core of everything he teaches is the Connection Expansion System™, which has since generated millions in sales for both him and the sales teams he's mentored over the last decade.

Imagine The Power Of 1,000,000 Connections

Reflecting on all the conversations I've had over the years, I could probably fill an entire book with stories about the impact that one connection has had on hundreds of individuals and businesses. It's what inspires me to equip more people with the Connection

Expansion System™ so we can continue to exponentially expand the collective impact that we are all having in the world.

Join A.C.E.S. - Amplified Connection Expansion Society

If you are looking for a fast-track to implementing the Connection Expansion System™ and increasing the quality of the connections you are receiving, I invite you to join the A.C.E.S. The Amplified Connection Expansion Society is a mastermind group that is 100% focused on building high-value connections for other members in the group. This is not your typical "networking" or "referral" group. This is a group of high-impact individuals who follow the core principles of the Connection Expansion System™ and are focused on helping uncover many-to-many relationships for themselves and the other members of the group.

In addition, this is the only way to gain ongoing access to my ever-growing network. While I always strive to add value to everyone I meet, this allows me to focus my attention on those who have prioritized this strategy as a core aspect of their personal and business success. Visit www.ConnectionExpansion.com to learn more.

CONCLUSION

If you've made it through this book, my hope for you is that you have a fresh perspective on the connections you already have and a new, strategic approach to building future relationships. I would love nothing more than to hear your story— about that one connection that opened up an opportunity you didn't think was possible.

In fact, as you implement the Connection Expansion System™ you can email any questions or success stories to info@ConnectionExpansionBook.com.

I am excited for you to finally have a duplicatable system that will help you build a high-value network, generating consistent new connections. This system will ultimately lead to predictable referrals for both you and your business. It's time for you to scale beyond the 5% of engaged customers who refer to your business and to find the *real value* that lies within your network.

Big Results From Unexpected Places

One of my favorite stories is about a very successful business owner who owns multiple seven-figure businesses. He found that he was getting stricter with his calendar and more protective of his time, yet wanted to seek out larger opportunities and partnerships. We were introduced by a mutual connection who believed I could help him with these goals.

During our first meeting, I told him that the types of connections I make may not make sense at first, but to trust the process. Following our Connection Meeting, I made 6 connections for him. His first response when he looked at the people I was connecting him with was to push back and say that I was wasting his time. I reminded him of our conversation and to trust the process. He followed through and booked meetings with the 6 connections. To his surprise, two opportunities emerged: one to acquire a company and another for a joint venture, together worth well into eight figures.

I love this story because it goes back to the idea that there is value in every relationship. Sometimes you have to stop making assumptions and just be curious. You never know where that next high-value relationship will come from!

What would your life or business look like if you consistently had new prospects being connected to you? New referral partners knocking at your door? Invitations for speaking engagements or podcast guesting? Connections for new strategic partnerships or joint venture opportunities? Introductions to highly aligned team members? Solving problems quickly and more affordably than you thought possible? Or any number of other amazing results that come from building a high-value network?

As you begin your journey, remember that one connection can get things started. Anything more will exponentially increase your outcome.

Remember to follow these core principles so that you can achieve your desired results:

- Always Add Value
- Control What You Can Control
- There Is Value In Every Relationship
- Never Make Assumptions About A Connection
- You Have To Train By Doing

I would hate to see you put this book down and go back to doing things the way you always have. You, your business, your employees, your family, your community, and everyone else that you impact deserve so much more. Remember, you are only one connection away from massive success in your life or business!

ABOUT THE AUTHOR

Driven by a passion for meaningful experiences, both personally and professionally, Devin Sizemore has spent his career building and growing businesses that align with his values. From launching his first marketing agency right out of college to creating innovative consulting practices and a cat cafe, his journey has been defined by a commitment to "adding value" and making a positive impact. As a firm believer in the power of connections, he is dedicated to helping others succeed through the art of building relationships. The next chapter of his life is focused on fostering a community where one million connections can create lasting, transformative change.

Made in the USA
Middletown, DE
25 March 2025

73198834R00066